A Man in Parts

Pianta

For all the places we've loved and wanted to hold on to

INTRODUCTION

Some places strike us in ways that are so unexpected that we have to return to them to see who we might be under their influence.

Introduction

A Poem in 8 parts

1. A Man In Parts

2. The Duomo

3. Beauty Apparent

4. Somewhere Else

5. The Tradesman Is Waiting

6. Certainty Eludes Him

7. His Own Form

8. One Last Time

Acknowledgments

A MAN IN PARTS

1.

a man in parts
wants to dismantle the life he leads
tired of engines that break
valves and smoke
and mufflers that flake into rust

he begins to undo
himself little by little
through carelessness
allowing himself to eye
cheap copies of tour flights
"Vanuatu ... The New Tahiti."
"Getaways! Paris! London! Rome!"

he appraises his bank account
like a climber gauging walls upon which he must rise

he asserts himself in the confines of his shower
forcing the water to cleanse the deep fascia and
subscapularis
worn from days of machine oil and heavy lifting

he rotates his head slowly
and the shower circles with him
cutting like a laser
a halo of steam

THE DUOMO

2.

it's upon entry of the Duomo
he first turns flush
his eyes falling upon the pink hued marble
he feels close to a prayer

later he looks through a window as his tour bus pulls away
his new religion—this pane of glass
he struggles to hold on to
the silhouetted lion's head baked to the tile
the copulas in Bologna that he strained his neck to see
and the small black shoes of Michelangelo's
in the Florence house
encased in a tidy clear cube

BEAUTY APPARENT

3.

during the meal with his companions
he doesn't discuss what thoughts come next
or the rush of the senses

giddy
he sits by himself
his heart beating
his legs slack
his stomach churning over

now he understands the romance
of the chisel, brush, or adz
and why bronze doors can warrant 500 years

even in dim light
beauty is apparent

but it's the immediacy of his own life
that staggers him
why he has loved the fitting together of pieces
and the workings of metal to metal
and his tears fall in a divine rush
that bless his corporeal flesh

SOMEWHERE ELSE

4.

he's sullen today
weeks later back home
the inevitability of his life burdens him

he waits at the DMV
glancing at his will-call ticket
watching the closed-circuit screen bounce with numbers
he looks at the registration form
and warps it into an arch
a doorway leading to somewhere else

his body arranged in an architecture of Vs
both forearms resting on his thighs
his head centered as if bowing
to the folding arc in his hands
he waits, hunched,
like a panther trapped in stone

THE TRADESMAN IS WAITING

5.

he's left the small apartment
the auto shop and congested beach street

his anxiousness about the move
has slimmed him
he's no longer bullish
but young and lithe

he waits at the airline gate
for his flight to be called
scanning the departure time for a place
he doesn't yet know

on the receiving end
the tradesman who has hired him smokes
leaning against the baggage cart
at the farthest edge of the tarmac
away from the flight supervisor's eye
he waits for the ground crew to clear
aloof but slightly unsteady, waiting
for the man of parts to arrive

the tradesman's eyes appear neutral
and unattached to the broad taxonomy of his type:
he, himself, has
worked on a plane—a barge—a hoist
or a crank shaft when it has been broken

or on oiled blades that have sharply twisted
before they've risen into air

he has lived long enough to shape glass
or forge steel into the shape of a woman
such work assembled disassembled
worshiped or tossed
he knows it's the rare case
when a man who can do this work chooses to stay

he'll see what this new one can do

CERTAINTY ELUDES HIM

6.

weeks later the man himself is broken into parts
sure yet unsure about why he has come
to a place whose language he doesn't know

the days have passed and certainty eludes him
despite the beauty and the changes he sought and found
despite the windows that open to fields
embellished with monasteries
or the backdrop of butter-colored stone
winding through hillsides—
or the long-legged strides of women
with dark hair in fitted coats
and their taut leather heels

he stirs at night
uneasy about the rural coast
where he ventures out on brief tours
they are as green-blue as the cove in his home town
but the damp keeps him sluggish and low

he keeps waiting for sunlight to touch his body
but the entrapment of wool and damp cling to him
both clammy and rough
so he resigns himself to the inevitability of culture shock
allowing himself the lure of excessive sleep
as thick as blood

like a dead man face down and drifting
he floats longer and longer into the lean shafts of morning
missing work, food and
the sounds of women coming up from the street
the faces impenetrable to him
and the language beautiful but elusive
never fitting in his mouth or lips

so much so that even the women he loves
look at him as he eats
as if studying traits they rarely see
he can't argue nor love with much precision
and without words what they have easily ebbs away

he sits and feels scrambled looking at the machinery
the parts and weights so different
and the order systems seems to jab parts of his brain
that he can't reach

the timetables strange and amorphous
the clocks irrelevant and impotent
in the face of human situations
and the breakdown of diesel deliveries

his face looks unfamiliar
to himself when he wakes one morning
so surprisingly unsure, uncomfortable, ill-suited to this
place

HIS OWN FORM

7.

he goes to the cathedrals and sits in the dark
his own form of communion
his eyes take in the curve of the chipped marble
and geometry of beams

this comforts him and when he steps out into the piazza
he feels cleaner
and delves again into the work and noise of the city

but months later over coffee
he tells them no, no,
he has to go home

the tradesman who hired him is silent
and doesn't argue against it like the rest of the crew
he's grown to respect his work and the man himself
so he doesn't counter and instead
merely pencils in the day of his departure
and watches him as he uncoils chains for the next hoist

ONE LAST TIME

8.

the day he leaves
he walks past the wooden fruit stalls
and the packed pastry shops
over the uneven stones of the street
and coming up from the station
he faces the cathedrals
to absorb them one last time

he aches and is humbled
he vows not to forget them
as he leaves them behind

on the airplane home
his legs throb in the cramped space
he feels crude and clumsy
but as he flies over the coastline
he sees the white caps
the beaches crisp and yellow
he taps the glass
and whistles at the sleek metal wing of the plane
when the sudden return of blue sky
sears him like a welder's torch

it melds him whole again
and in the absence of any separateness
his attention feels attached and unattached
and he wonders
if this is what it's like
to love
yet be free

ACKNOWLEDGMENTS

Much gratitude to friends and family for always supporting me, and special appreciation to Simone and Guido and their families for being so gracious all those years ago. It's that kind of kindness that makes places and people unforgettable.

ABOUT THE AUTHOR

Pianta is a writer and editor whose work has appeared in journals such as *Nimrod International Journal*, *Adirondack Review*, *Ekphrasis*, *Terrain.org*, and *Bamboo Ridge Press*. Originally from O'ahu, she now lives on the Big Island of Hawai'i. Her readings often incorporate live music, dance, and multimedia. Her website can be found at www.pianta.org.

CURRENT RELEASES

Hawai'i Poems: from there to here
Collection of new and previously published poems
Available on Apple Books

Little Bird: Songs for Children
CD of children's songs
Available on iTunes and Apple Music
Samples at
https://pianta.hearnow.com/

Old Volcano Road
Novella
Ebook and print versions
Available on Kindle and Amazon

We Don't Know What We Don't Know
Poetry chapbook
Print version available on Amazon

All Ends Never End
Poetry chapbook
Print version available on Amazon

Acts and Intentions
Poetry chapbook
Print version on Amazon

Love and Grief in the Time of Ketu
Poetry chapbook
Print version on Amazon

Before
Poetry chapbook

Short fiction

Floating
Ebook on Apple Books
Print version on Amazon

For more information
www.pianta.org

www.ingramcontent.com/pod-product-compliance
Lightning Source LLC
Chambersburg PA
CBHW060556030426
42337CB00019B/3559